Taming You.

A Journal to Help with Daily Reflection, to Refocus, and Find Balance Between a Stressful Life and Personal Care.

Taming Your Inner Lion Journal

A Journal to Help with Daily Reflection, to Refocus, and Find Balance Between a Stressful Life and Personal Care.

D Smart

25/8 Media and Publication

ISBN 978-0-578-61420-5

Manufactured in the USA

First Edition

The information presented in this journal is for supplemental assistance. Seeking a trained professional for any perceived issues, psychological struggles, or mental issues is recommended.

This journal was created to help you keep track of stressors you have and what may trigger them, to better find balance in your life. It is also a tracker to see how balanced your life is between what you do for others and the time you take for personal care of yourself. The old cliché of the emergency on an airplane and having to put your air mask on first before helping others, is relevant. I have provided tips, numbers, and resources to help you on your journey of living a healthy, balanced, and fulfilling life. The pages are setup for you to answer daily questions by bubbling the answer, but if you are dealing with high stress on a daily basis, take time to write what you are doing or how you feel next to each task. For example, for caring for/helping someone you can write I took my elderly neighbor to the store for an hour. For stress levels you can circle more than one choice if you feel you are entering into another stress level. For received counseling, it can   be a professional or a good friend who you were able to talk out how you were feeling. For were you physically active, if you have mobility issues you can document that you stretched. For free thought, you can write whatever comes to mind on that day. For me I like to write down dreams or projects or ideas I would like to pursue at some point. My favorite part is the daily quote/mantra/and or Bible verse because it can be your rallying cry each day.

This journal is setup to the best of my ability to capture everyone's schedule if you are a person who works Sunday-Wednesday, Wednesday-Sunday, 7am start of day, 12am start of your night, or anything in between.

The goal of this journal is to help you keep yourself balanced or work toward finding balance and coping skills, in your life.

Thank you

Date_____

What You Face in Your Territory Today/Tonight:

What are you most stressed about at the start of your day/night?

_____

_____

_____

Work/Overtime/and/or Side Job o

_____

_____

_____

Caring for/Helping Someone o

_____

_____

_____

_____

Helping/Assisting Family o

_____

_____

_____

_____

Housework/Doing Errands o

_____

_____

_____

Other Tasks/Other Things You Did o

_____

_____

_____

Paying Bills o

_____

_____

Groups/Organizations/Committees o

_____

_____

_____

_____

_____

Volunteering/Charity/Kind Acts o

_____

_____

_____

Something Good That Happened/Something You Want to Vent About o

_____

_____

_____

_____

_____

_____

_____

_____

_____

_____

Personal Check-in

Daily Quote/Mantra/and/ or Bible Versus for Motivation or Mood You Are In:

_____

_____

_____

_____

_____

_____

_____

_____

Hours of Sleep You Had Last Night/Day:

_____

Was Physically Active o

_____

Ate Balanced Meals o

_____

_____

Took Prescribed Medication/Received Counseling o

_____

_____

Able to Put Money Toward Savings o

_____

Did Something Relaxing o

_____

Saw Something Amazing o

Stress Level at the End of the Day/Night: Calm, Medium, On the Verge, High

What is Placing You at That Level:

_____

_____

_____

_____

_____

Other Thoughts of the Day/Night

_____

_____

_____

_____

Date: _____

Stress Level Monitor During Your Day/Night

Stress Level: Calm/Medium/On the Verge/High

Time of Stress

_____

Place of Stress

_____

What You Were Doing

_____

Who You Were With

_____

How You Felt Physically During Your Stressful Moment

_____

_____

How You Felt Emotionally During Your Stressful Moment

_____

_____

Were You Able to Cope? Yes or No/ How Did You Cope?

_____

_____

Date: _____

Stress Level Monitor During Your Day/Night

Stress Level: Calm/Medium/On the Verge/High

Time of Stress

_____

Place of Stress

_____

What You Were Doing

_____

Who You Were With

_____

How You Felt Physically During Your Stressful Moment

_____

_____

How You Felt Emotionally During Your Stressful
Moment

_____

_____

Were You Able to Cope? Yes or No/ How Did You
Cope?

_____

_____

_____

Date: _____

Stress Level Monitor During Your Day/Night

Stress Level: Calm/Medium/On the Verge/High

Time of Stress

_____

Place of Stress

_____

What You Were Doing

_____

Who You Were With

_____

How You Felt Physically During Your Stressful Moment

_____

_____

How You Felt Emotionally During Your Stressful
Moment

_____

_____

Were You Able to Cope? Yes or No/ How Did You
Cope?

_____

_____

_____

Date: _____

Stress Level Monitor During Your Day/Night

Stress Level: Calm/Medium/On the Verge/High

Time of Stress

_____

Place of Stress

_____

What You Were Doing

_____

Who You Were With

_____

How You Felt Physically During Your Stressful Moment

_____

_____

How You Felt Emotionally During Your Stressful
Moment

_____

_____

Were You Able to Cope? Yes or No/ How Did You
Cope? _____

_____

_____

Free Thought Page

_____

_____

_____

_____

_____

_____

_____

_____

_____

_____

_____

_____

_____

_____

_____

_____

_____

_____

_____

_____

_____

_____

_____

_____

_____

Date_____

What You Face in Your Territory Today/Tonight:

What are you most stressed about at the start of your day/night?

_____

_____

_____

Work/Overtime/and/or Side Job o

_____

_____

_____

Caring for/Helping Someone o

_____

_____

_____

_____

Helping/Assisting Family o

_____

_____

_____

_____

Housework/Doing Errands o

_____

_____

_____

Other Tasks/Other Things You Did o

_____

_____

_____

Paying Bills o

_____

_____

Groups/Organizations/Committees o

_____

_____

_____

_____

_____

Volunteering/Charity/Kind Acts o

_____

_____

_____

Something Good That Happened/Something You Want
to Vent About o

_____

_____

_____

_____

_____

_____

_____

_____

_____

_____

Personal Check-in

Daily Quote/Mantra/and/ or Bible Versus for Motivation or Mood You Are In:

_____

_____

_____

_____

_____

_____

_____

_____

Hours of Sleep You Had Last Night/Day:

_____

Was Physically Active o

_____

Ate Balanced Meals o

_____

_____

Took Prescribed Medication/Received Counseling o

_____

_____

Able to Put Money Toward Savings o

_____

Did Something Relaxing o

_____

Saw Something Amazing o

_____

Stress Level at the End of the Day/Night: Calm, Medium, On the Verge, High

What is Placing You at That Level:

_____

_____

_____

_____

_____

Other Thoughts of the Day/Night

_____

_____

_____

_____

Date: _____

Stress Level Monitor During Your Day/Night

Stress Level: Calm/Medium/On the Verge/High

Time of Stress

_____

Place of Stress

_____

What You Were Doing

_____

Who You Were With

_____

How You Felt Physically During Your Stressful Moment

_____

_____

How You Felt Emotionally During Your Stressful
Moment

_____

_____

Were You Able to Cope? Yes or No/ How Did You
Cope?

_____

_____

_____

Date: _____

Stress Level Monitor During Your Day/Night

Stress Level: Calm/Medium/On the Verge/High

Time of Stress

_____

Place of Stress

_____

What You Were Doing

_____

Who You Were With

_____

How You Felt Physically During Your Stressful Moment

_____

_____

How You Felt Emotionally During Your Stressful Moment

_____

_____

Were You Able to Cope? Yes or No/ How Did You Cope?

_____

_____

_____

Date: _____

Stress Level Monitor During Your Day/Night

Stress Level: Calm/Medium/On the Verge/High

Time of Stress

_____

Place of Stress

_____

What You Were Doing

_____

Who You Were With

_____

How You Felt Physically During Your Stressful Moment

_____

_____

How You Felt Emotionally During Your Stressful Moment

_____

_____

Were You Able to Cope? Yes or No/ How Did You Cope?

_____

_____

_____

Date: _____

Stress Level Monitor During Your Day/Night

Stress Level: Calm/Medium/On the Verge/High

Time of Stress

_____

Place of Stress

_____

What You Were Doing

_____

Who You Were With

_____

How You Felt Physically During Your Stressful Moment

_____

_____

How You Felt Emotionally During Your Stressful
Moment

_____

_____

Were You Able to Cope? Yes or No/ How Did You
Cope? _____

_____

_____

Free Thought Page

Date_____

What You Face in Your Territory Today/Tonight:

What are you most stressed about at the start of your day/night?

_____
_____
_____

Work/Overtime/and/or Side Job o

_____
_____
_____

Caring for/Helping Someone o

_____
_____
_____
_____

Helping/Assisting Family o

_____
_____
_____
_____

Housework/Doing Errands o

_____
_____
_____

Other Tasks/Other Things You Did o

_____

_____

_____

Paying Bills o

_____

_____

Groups/Organizations/Committees o

_____

_____

_____

_____

_____

Volunteering/Charity/Kind Acts o

_____

_____

_____

Something Good That Happened/Something You Want to Vent About o

_____

_____

_____

_____

_____

_____

_____

_____

_____

_____

Personal Check-in

Daily Quote/Mantra/and/ or Bible Versus for Motivation or Mood You Are In:

_____

_____

_____

_____

_____

_____

_____

Hours of Sleep You Had Last Night/Day:

_____

Was Physically Active o

_____

Ate Balanced Meals o

_____

_____

Took Prescribed Medication/Received Counseling o

_____

_____

Able to Put Money Toward Savings o

_____

Did Something Relaxing o

_____

Saw Something Amazing o

Stress Level at the End of the Day/Night: Calm, Medium, On the Verge, High

What is Placing You at That Level:

_____

_____

_____

_____

_____

Other Thoughts of the Day/Night

_____

_____

_____

_____

_____

Date: _____

Stress Level Monitor During Your Day/Night

Stress Level: Calm/Medium/On the Verge/High

Time of Stress

_____

Place of Stress

_____

What You Were Doing

_____

Who You Were With

_____

How You Felt Physically During Your Stressful Moment

_____

_____

How You Felt Emotionally During Your Stressful Moment

_____

_____

Were You Able to Cope? Yes or No/ How Did You Cope?

_____

_____

_____

Date: _____

Stress Level Monitor During Your Day/Night

Stress Level: Calm/Medium/On the Verge/High

Time of Stress

_____

Place of Stress

_____

What You Were Doing

_____

Who You Were With

_____

How You Felt Physically During Your Stressful Moment

_____

_____

How You Felt Emotionally During Your Stressful
Moment

_____

_____

Were You Able to Cope? Yes or No/ How Did You
Cope?

_____

_____

_____

Date: _____

Stress Level Monitor During Your Day/Night

Stress Level: Calm/Medium/On the Verge/High

Time of Stress

_____

Place of Stress

_____

What You Were Doing

_____

Who You Were With

_____

How You Felt Physically During Your Stressful Moment

_____

_____

How You Felt Emotionally During Your Stressful Moment

_____

_____

Were You Able to Cope? Yes or No/ How Did You Cope?

_____

_____

_____

Date: _____

Stress Level Monitor During Your Day/Night

Stress Level: Calm/Medium/On the Verge/High

Time of Stress

_____

Place of Stress

_____

What You Were Doing

_____

Who You Were With

_____

How You Felt Physically During Your Stressful Moment

_____

_____

How You Felt Emotionally During Your Stressful
Moment

_____

_____

Were You Able to Cope? Yes or No/ How Did You
Cope? _____

_____

_____

Free Thought Page

_____

_____

_____

_____

_____

_____

_____

_____

_____

_____

_____

_____

_____

_____

_____

_____

_____

_____

_____

_____

_____

_____

_____

_____

_____

Date_____

What You Face in Your Territory Today/Tonight:

What are you most stressed about at the start of your day/night?

_____
_____
_____

Work/Overtime/and/or Side Job o

_____
_____
_____

Caring for/Helping Someone o

_____
_____
_____
_____

Helping/Assisting Family o

_____
_____
_____
_____

Housework/Doing Errands o

_____
_____
_____

Other Tasks/Other Things You Did o

_____

_____

_____

Paying Bills o

_____

_____

Groups/Organizations/Committees o

_____

_____

_____

_____

Volunteering/Charity/Kind Acts o

_____

_____

_____

Something Good That Happened/Something You Want to Vent About o

_____

_____

_____

_____

_____

_____

_____

_____

_____

_____

Personal Check-in

Daily Quote/Mantra/and/ or Bible Versus for
Motivation or Mood You Are In:

_____

_____

_____

_____

_____

_____

_____

_____

Hours of Sleep You Had Last Night/Day:

_____

Was Physically Active o

_____

Ate Balanced Meals o

_____

_____

Took Prescribed Medication/Received Counseling o

_____

_____

Able to Put Money Toward Savings o

_____

Did Something Relaxing o

_____

Saw Something Amazing o

Stress Level at the End of the Day/Night: Calm, Medium, On the Verge, High

What is Placing You at That Level:

_____

_____

_____

_____

_____

Other Thoughts of the Day/Night

_____

_____

_____

_____

_____

Date: _____

Stress Level Monitor During Your Day/Night

Stress Level: Calm/Medium/On the Verge/High

Time of Stress

_____

Place of Stress

_____

What You Were Doing

_____

Who You Were With

_____

How You Felt Physically During Your Stressful Moment

_____

_____

How You Felt Emotionally During Your Stressful Moment

_____

_____

Were You Able to Cope? Yes or No/ How Did You Cope?

_____

_____

_____

Date: _____

Stress Level Monitor During Your Day/Night

Stress Level: Calm/Medium/On the Verge/High

Time of Stress

_____

Place of Stress

_____

What You Were Doing

_____

Who You Were With

_____

How You Felt Physically During Your Stressful Moment

_____

_____

How You Felt Emotionally During Your Stressful Moment

_____

_____

Were You Able to Cope? Yes or No/ How Did You Cope?

_____

_____

_____

Date: _____

Stress Level Monitor During Your Day/Night

Stress Level: Calm/Medium/On the Verge/High

Time of Stress

_____

Place of Stress

_____

What You Were Doing

_____

Who You Were With

_____

How You Felt Physically During Your Stressful Moment

_____

_____

How You Felt Emotionally During Your Stressful
Moment

_____

_____

Were You Able to Cope? Yes or No/ How Did You
Cope?

_____

_____

_____

Date: _____

Stress Level Monitor During Your Day/Night

Stress Level: Calm/Medium/On the Verge/High

Time of Stress

_____

Place of Stress

_____

What You Were Doing

_____

Who You Were With

_____

How You Felt Physically During Your Stressful Moment

_____

_____

How You Felt Emotionally During Your Stressful
Moment

_____

_____

Were You Able to Cope? Yes or No/ How Did You
Cope? _____

_____

_____

Free Thought Page

_____

_____

_____

_____

_____

_____

_____

_____

_____

_____

_____

_____

_____

_____

_____

_____

_____

_____

_____

_____

_____

_____

_____

_____

_____

_____

_____

_____

_____

_____

_____

_____

_____

_____

Date_____

What You Face in Your Territory Today/Tonight:

What are you most stressed about at the start of your day/night?

_____

_____

_____

Work/Overtime/and/or Side Job o

_____

_____

_____

Caring for/Helping Someone o

_____

_____

_____

_____

Helping/Assisting Family o

_____

_____

_____

_____

Housework/Doing Errands o

_____

_____

_____

Other Tasks/Other Things You Did o

_____

_____

_____

Paying Bills o

_____

_____

Groups/Organizations/Committees o

_____

_____

_____

_____

_____

Volunteering/Charity/Kind Acts o

_____

_____

_____

Something Good That Happened/Something You Want to Vent About o

_____

_____

_____

_____

_____

_____

_____

_____

_____

_____

Personal Check-in

Daily Quote/Mantra/and/ or Bible Versus for
Motivation or Mood You Are In:

_____

_____

_____

_____

_____

_____

_____

_____

Hours of Sleep You Had Last Night/Day:

_____

Was Physically Active o

_____

Ate Balanced Meals o

_____

_____

Took Prescribed Medication/Received Counseling o

_____

_____

Able to Put Money Toward Savings o

_____

Did Something Relaxing o

_____

Saw Something Amazing o

_____

Stress Level at the End of the Day/Night: Calm, Medium,
On the Verge, High

What is Placing You at That Level:

_____

_____

_____

_____

_____

Other Thoughts of the Day/Night

_____

_____

_____

_____

_____

Date: _____

Stress Level Monitor During Your Day/Night

Stress Level: Calm/Medium/On the Verge/High

Time of Stress

_____

Place of Stress

_____

What You Were Doing

_____

Who You Were With

_____

How You Felt Physically During Your Stressful Moment

_____

_____

How You Felt Emotionally During Your Stressful Moment

_____

_____

Were You Able to Cope? Yes or No/ How Did You Cope?

_____

_____

_____

Date: _____

Stress Level Monitor During Your Day/Night

Stress Level: Calm/Medium/On the Verge/High

Time of Stress

_____

Place of Stress

_____

What You Were Doing

_____

Who You Were With

_____

How You Felt Physically During Your Stressful Moment

_____

_____

How You Felt Emotionally During Your Stressful
Moment

_____

_____

Were You Able to Cope? Yes or No/ How Did You
Cope?

_____

_____

_____

Date: _____

Stress Level Monitor During Your Day/Night

Stress Level: Calm/Medium/On the Verge/High

Time of Stress

_____

Place of Stress

_____

What You Were Doing

_____

Who You Were With

_____

How You Felt Physically During Your Stressful Moment

_____
_____

How You Felt Emotionally During Your Stressful Moment

_____

_____

Were You Able to Cope? Yes or No/ How Did You Cope?

_____

_____

_____

Date: _____

Stress Level Monitor During Your Day/Night

Stress Level: Calm/Medium/On the Verge/High

Time of Stress

_____

Place of Stress

_____

What You Were Doing

_____

Who You Were With

_____

How You Felt Physically During Your Stressful Moment

_____

_____

How You Felt Emotionally During Your Stressful
Moment

_____

_____

Were You Able to Cope? Yes or No/ How Did You
Cope? _____

_____

_____

Free Thought Page

_____

_____

_____

_____

_____

_____

_____

_____

_____

_____

_____

_____

_____

_____

_____

_____

_____

_____

_____

_____

_____

_____

_____

_____

_____

_____

Date_____

What You Face in Your Territory Today/Tonight:

What are you most stressed about at the start of your day/night?

_____
_____
_____

Work/Overtime/and/or Side Job o

_____
_____
_____

Caring for/Helping Someone o

_____
_____
_____
_____

Helping/Assisting Family o

_____
_____
_____
_____

Housework/Doing Errands o

_____
_____
_____

Other Tasks/Other Things You Did o

_____

_____

_____

Paying Bills o

_____

_____

Groups/Organizations/Committees o

_____

_____

_____

_____

Volunteering/Charity/Kind Acts o

_____

_____

_____

Something Good That Happened/Something You Want
to Vent About o

_____

_____

_____

_____

_____

_____

_____

_____

_____

_____

Personal Check-in

Daily Quote/Mantra/and/ or Bible Versus for Motivation or Mood You Are In:

_____

_____

_____

_____

_____

_____

_____

_____

Hours of Sleep You Had Last Night/Day:

_____

Was Physically Active o

_____

Ate Balanced Meals o

_____

_____

Took Prescribed Medication/Received Counseling o

_____

_____

Able to Put Money Toward Savings o

_____

Did Something Relaxing o

_____

Saw Something Amazing o

Stress Level at the End of the Day/Night: Calm, Medium, On the Verge, High

What is Placing You at That Level:

_____

_____

_____

_____

_____

Other Thoughts of the Day/Night

_____

_____

_____

_____

Date: _____

Stress Level Monitor During Your Day/Night

Stress Level: Calm/Medium/On the Verge/High

Time of Stress

_____

Place of Stress

_____

What You Were Doing

_____

Who You Were With

_____

How You Felt Physically During Your Stressful Moment

_____

_____

How You Felt Emotionally During Your Stressful Moment

_____

_____

Were You Able to Cope? Yes or No/ How Did You Cope?

_____

_____

Date: _____

Stress Level Monitor During Your Day/Night

Stress Level: Calm/Medium/On the Verge/High

Time of Stress

_____

Place of Stress

_____

What You Were Doing

_____

Who You Were With

_____

How You Felt Physically During Your Stressful Moment

_____

_____

How You Felt Emotionally During Your Stressful Moment

_____

_____

Were You Able to Cope? Yes or No/ How Did You Cope?

_____

_____

_____

Date: _____

Stress Level Monitor During Your Day/Night

Stress Level: Calm/Medium/On the Verge/High

Time of Stress

_____

Place of Stress

_____

What You Were Doing

_____

Who You Were With

_____

How You Felt Physically During Your Stressful Moment

_____

_____

How You Felt Emotionally During Your Stressful
Moment

_____

_____

Were You Able to Cope? Yes or No/ How Did You
Cope?

_____

_____

_____

Date: _____

Stress Level Monitor During Your Day/Night

Stress Level: Calm/Medium/On the Verge/High

Time of Stress

_____

Place of Stress

_____

What You Were Doing

_____

Who You Were With

_____

How You Felt Physically During Your Stressful Moment

_____

_____

How You Felt Emotionally During Your Stressful
Moment

_____

_____

Were You Able to Cope? Yes or No/ How Did You
Cope? _____

_____

_____

Free Thought Page

Date_____

What You Face in Your Territory Today/Tonight:

What are you most stressed about at the start of your day/night?

_____
_____
_____

Work/Overtime/and/or Side Job o

_____
_____
_____

Caring for/Helping Someone o

_____
_____
_____
_____

Helping/Assisting Family o

_____
_____
_____
_____

Housework/Doing Errands o

_____
_____
_____

Other Tasks/Other Things You Did o

_____

_____

_____

Paying Bills o

_____

_____

Groups/Organizations/Committees o

_____

_____

_____

_____

_____

Volunteering/Charity/Kind Acts o

_____

_____

_____

Something Good That Happened/Something You Want
to Vent About o

_____

_____

_____

_____

_____

_____

_____

_____

_____

_____

Personal Check-in

Daily Quote/Mantra/and/ or Bible Versus for
Motivation or Mood You Are In:

_____

_____

_____

_____

_____

_____

_____

_____

Hours of Sleep You Had Last Night/Day:

_____

Was Physically Active o

_____

Ate Balanced Meals o

_____

_____

Took Prescribed Medication/Received Counseling o

_____

_____

Able to Put Money Toward Savings o

_____

Did Something Relaxing o

_____

Saw Something Amazing o

Stress Level at the End of the Day/Night: Calm, Medium, On the Verge, High

What is Placing You at That Level:

_____

_____

_____

_____

_____

Other Thoughts of the Day/Night

_____

_____

_____

_____

Date: _____

Stress Level Monitor During Your Day/Night

Stress Level: Calm/Medium/On the Verge/High

Time of Stress

_____

Place of Stress

_____

What You Were Doing

_____

Who You Were With

_____

How You Felt Physically During Your Stressful Moment

_____

_____

How You Felt Emotionally During Your Stressful
Moment

_____

_____

Were You Able to Cope? Yes or No/ How Did You
Cope?

_____

_____

_____

Date: _____

Stress Level Monitor During Your Day/Night

Stress Level: Calm/Medium/On the Verge/High

Time of Stress

_____

Place of Stress

_____

What You Were Doing

_____

Who You Were With

_____

How You Felt Physically During Your Stressful Moment

_____

_____

How You Felt Emotionally During Your Stressful Moment

_____

_____

Were You Able to Cope? Yes or No/ How Did You Cope?

_____

_____

_____

Date: _____

Stress Level Monitor During Your Day/Night

Stress Level: Calm/Medium/On the Verge/High

Time of Stress

_____

Place of Stress

_____

What You Were Doing

_____

Who You Were With

_____

How You Felt Physically During Your Stressful Moment

_____

_____

How You Felt Emotionally During Your Stressful
Moment

_____

_____

Were You Able to Cope? Yes or No/ How Did You
Cope?

_____

_____

_____

Date: _____

Stress Level Monitor During Your Day/Night

Stress Level: Calm/Medium/On the Verge/High

Time of Stress

_____

Place of Stress

_____

What You Were Doing

_____

Who You Were With

_____

How You Felt Physically During Your Stressful Moment

_____

_____

How You Felt Emotionally During Your Stressful
Moment

_____

_____

Were You Able to Cope? Yes or No/ How Did You
Cope? _____

_____

_____

Free Thought Page

Date_____

What You Face in Your Territory Today/Tonight:

What are you most stressed about at the start of your day/night?

_____

_____

_____

Work/Overtime/and/or Side Job o

_____

_____

_____

Caring for/Helping Someone o

_____

_____

_____

_____

Helping/Assisting Family o

_____

_____

_____

_____

Housework/Doing Errands o

_____

_____

_____

Other Tasks/Other Things You Did o

_____

_____

_____

Paying Bills o

_____

_____

Groups/Organizations/Committees o

_____

_____

_____

_____

_____

Volunteering/Charity/Kind Acts o

_____

_____

_____

Something Good That Happened/Something You Want
to Vent About o

_____

_____

_____

_____

_____

_____

_____

_____

_____

_____

Personal Check-in

Daily Quote/Mantra/and/ or Bible Versus for
Motivation or Mood You Are In:

_____

_____

_____

_____

_____

_____

_____

_____

Hours of Sleep You Had Last Night/Day:

_____

Was Physically Active o

_____

Ate Balanced Meals o

_____

_____

Took Prescribed Medication/Received Counseling o

_____

_____

Able to Put Money Toward Savings o

_____

Did Something Relaxing o

_____

Saw Something Amazing o

_____

Stress Level at the End of the Day/Night: Calm, Medium,
On the Verge, High

What is Placing You at That Level:

_____

_____

_____

_____

_____

Other Thoughts of the Day/Night

_____

_____

_____

_____

_____

Date: _____

Stress Level Monitor During Your Day/Night

Stress Level: Calm/Medium/On the Verge/High

Time of Stress

_____

Place of Stress

_____

What You Were Doing

_____

Who You Were With

_____

How You Felt Physically During Your Stressful Moment

_____

_____

How You Felt Emotionally During Your Stressful Moment

_____

_____

Were You Able to Cope? Yes or No/ How Did You Cope?

_____

_____

Date: _____

Stress Level Monitor During Your Day/Night

Stress Level: Calm/Medium/On the Verge/High

Time of Stress

_____

Place of Stress

_____

What You Were Doing

_____

Who You Were With

_____

How You Felt Physically During Your Stressful Moment

_____

_____

How You Felt Emotionally During Your Stressful Moment

_____

_____

Were You Able to Cope? Yes or No/ How Did You Cope?

_____

_____

_____

Date: _____

Stress Level Monitor During Your Day/Night

Stress Level: Calm/Medium/On the Verge/High

Time of Stress

_____

Place of Stress

_____

What You Were Doing

_____

Who You Were With

_____

How You Felt Physically During Your Stressful Moment

_____

_____

How You Felt Emotionally During Your Stressful Moment

_____

_____

Were You Able to Cope? Yes or No/ How Did You Cope?

_____

_____

_____

Date: _____

Stress Level Monitor During Your Day/Night

Stress Level: Calm/Medium/On the Verge/High

Time of Stress

_____

Place of Stress

_____

What You Were Doing

_____

Who You Were With

_____

How You Felt Physically During Your Stressful Moment

_____

_____

How You Felt Emotionally During Your Stressful Moment

_____

_____

Were You Able to Cope? Yes or No/ How Did You Cope? _____

_____

_____

Free Thought Page

_____

_____

_____

_____

_____

_____

_____

_____

_____

_____

_____

_____

_____

_____

_____

_____

_____

_____

_____

_____

_____

_____

_____

_____

_____

_____

_____

_____

_____

_____

_____

Date_____

What You Face in Your Territory Today/Tonight:

What are you most stressed about at the start of your day/night?

_____

_____

_____

Work/Overtime/and/or Side Job o

_____

_____

_____

Caring for/Helping Someone o

_____

_____

_____

_____

Helping/Assisting Family o

_____

_____

_____

_____

Housework/Doing Errands o

_____

_____

_____

Other Tasks/Other Things You Did o

_____

_____

_____

Paying Bills o

_____

_____

Groups/Organizations/Committees o

_____

_____

_____

_____

Volunteering/Charity/Kind Acts o

_____

_____

_____

Something Good That Happened/Something You Want to Vent About o

_____

_____

_____

_____

_____

_____

_____

_____

_____

_____

Personal Check-in

Daily Quote/Mantra/and/ or Bible Versus for
Motivation or Mood You Are In:

_____

_____

_____

_____

_____

_____

_____

Hours of Sleep You Had Last Night/Day:

_____

Was Physically Active o

_____

Ate Balanced Meals o

_____

Took Prescribed Medication/Received Counseling o

_____

Able to Put Money Toward Savings o

_____

Did Something Relaxing o

_____

Saw Something Amazing o

Stress Level at the End of the Day/Night: Calm, Medium, On the Verge, High

What is Placing You at That Level:

_____

_____

_____

_____

_____

Other Thoughts of the Day/Night

_____

_____

_____

_____

Date: _____

Stress Level Monitor During Your Day/Night

Stress Level: Calm/Medium/On the Verge/High

Time of Stress

_____

Place of Stress

_____

What You Were Doing

_____

Who You Were With

_____

How You Felt Physically During Your Stressful Moment

_____

_____

How You Felt Emotionally During Your Stressful Moment

_____

_____

Were You Able to Cope? Yes or No/ How Did You Cope?

_____

_____

_____

Date: _____

Stress Level Monitor During Your Day/Night

Stress Level: Calm/Medium/On the Verge/High

Time of Stress

_____

Place of Stress

_____

What You Were Doing

_____

Who You Were With

_____

How You Felt Physically During Your Stressful Moment

_____

_____

How You Felt Emotionally During Your Stressful
Moment

_____

_____

Were You Able to Cope? Yes or No/ How Did You
Cope?

_____

_____

_____

Date: _____

Stress Level Monitor During Your Day/Night

Stress Level: Calm/Medium/On the Verge/High

Time of Stress

_____

Place of Stress

_____

What You Were Doing

_____

Who You Were With

_____

How You Felt Physically During Your Stressful Moment

_____

_____

How You Felt Emotionally During Your Stressful
Moment

_____

_____

Were You Able to Cope? Yes or No/ How Did You
Cope?

_____

_____

_____

Date: _____

Stress Level Monitor During Your Day/Night

Stress Level: Calm/Medium/On the Verge/High

Time of Stress

_____

Place of Stress

_____

What You Were Doing

_____

Who You Were With

_____

How You Felt Physically During Your Stressful Moment

_____

_____

How You Felt Emotionally During Your Stressful
Moment

_____

_____

Were You Able to Cope? Yes or No/ How Did You
Cope? _____

_____

_____

Free Thought Page

Date_____

What You Face in Your Territory Today/Tonight:

What are you most stressed about at the start of your day/night?

_____

_____

_____

Work/Overtime/and/or Side Job o

_____

_____

_____

Caring for/Helping Someone o

_____

_____

_____

_____

Helping/Assisting Family o

_____

_____

_____

_____

Housework/Doing Errands o

_____

_____

_____

Other Tasks/Other Things You Did o

_____

_____
_____

Paying Bills o

_____
_____

Groups/Organizations/Committees o

_____
_____
_____
_____
_____

Volunteering/Charity/Kind Acts o

_____
_____
_____

Something Good That Happened/Something You Want
to Vent About o

_____
_____
_____
_____
_____
_____
_____
_____

_____

_____

Personal Check-in

Daily Quote/Mantra/and/ or Bible Versus for Motivation or Mood You Are In:

_____

_____

_____

_____

_____

_____

_____

_____

Hours of Sleep You Had Last Night/Day:

_____

Was Physically Active o

_____

Ate Balanced Meals o

_____

_____

Took Prescribed Medication/Received Counseling o

_____

_____

Able to Put Money Toward Savings o

_____

Did Something Relaxing o

_____

Saw Something Amazing o

Stress Level at the End of the Day/Night: Calm, Medium, On the Verge, High

What is Placing You at That Level:

_____

_____

_____

_____

_____

Other Thoughts of the Day/Night

_____

_____

_____

_____

Date: _____

Stress Level Monitor During Your Day/Night

Stress Level: Calm/Medium/On the Verge/High

Time of Stress

_____

Place of Stress

_____

What You Were Doing

_____

Who You Were With

_____

How You Felt Physically During Your Stressful Moment

_____

_____

How You Felt Emotionally During Your Stressful
Moment

_____

_____

Were You Able to Cope? Yes or No/ How Did You
Cope?

_____

_____

_____

Date: _____

Stress Level Monitor During Your Day/Night

Stress Level: Calm/Medium/On the Verge/High

Time of Stress

_____

Place of Stress

_____

What You Were Doing

_____

Who You Were With

_____

How You Felt Physically During Your Stressful Moment

_____

_____

How You Felt Emotionally During Your Stressful
Moment

_____

_____

Were You Able to Cope? Yes or No/ How Did You
Cope?

_____

_____

_____

Date: _____

Stress Level Monitor During Your Day/Night

Stress Level: Calm/Medium/On the Verge/High

Time of Stress

_____

Place of Stress

_____

What You Were Doing

_____

Who You Were With

_____

How You Felt Physically During Your Stressful Moment

_____

_____

How You Felt Emotionally During Your Stressful Moment

_____

_____

Were You Able to Cope? Yes or No/ How Did You Cope?

_____

_____

_____

Date: _____

Stress Level Monitor During Your Day/Night

Stress Level: Calm/Medium/On the Verge/High

Time of Stress

_____

Place of Stress

_____

What You Were Doing

_____

Who You Were With

_____

How You Felt Physically During Your Stressful Moment

_____

_____

How You Felt Emotionally During Your Stressful Moment

_____

_____

Were You Able to Cope? Yes or No/ How Did You Cope? _____

_____

_____

Free Thought Page

Date_____

What You Face in Your Territory Today/Tonight:

What are you most stressed about at the start of your day/night?

_____
_____
_____

Work/Overtime/and/or Side Job o

_____
_____
_____

Caring for/Helping Someone o

_____
_____
_____
_____

Helping/Assisting Family o

_____
_____
_____
_____

Housework/Doing Errands o

_____
_____
_____

Other Tasks/Other Things You Did o

_____

_____

_____

Paying Bills o

_____

_____

Groups/Organizations/Committees o

_____

_____

_____

_____

Volunteering/Charity/Kind Acts o

_____

_____

Something Good That Happened/Something You Want to Vent About o

_____

_____

_____

_____

_____

_____

_____

_____

_____

_____

Personal Check-in

Daily Quote/Mantra/and/ or Bible Versus for
Motivation or Mood You Are In:

_____

_____

_____

_____

_____

_____

_____

_____

Hours of Sleep You Had Last Night/Day:

_____

Was Physically Active o

_____

Ate Balanced Meals o

_____

_____

Took Prescribed Medication/Received Counseling o

_____

_____

Able to Put Money Toward Savings o

_____

Did Something Relaxing o

_____

Saw Something Amazing o

Stress Level at the End of the Day/Night: Calm, Medium, On the Verge, High

What is Placing You at That Level:

_____

_____

_____

_____

_____

Other Thoughts of the Day/Night

_____

_____

_____

_____

Date: _____

Stress Level Monitor During Your Day/Night

Stress Level: Calm/Medium/On the Verge/High

Time of Stress

_____

Place of Stress

_____

What You Were Doing

_____

Who You Were With

_____

How You Felt Physically During Your Stressful Moment

_____

_____

How You Felt Emotionally During Your Stressful Moment

_____

_____

Were You Able to Cope? Yes or No/ How Did You Cope?

_____

_____

_____

Date: _____

Stress Level Monitor During Your Day/Night

Stress Level: Calm/Medium/On the Verge/High

Time of Stress

_____

Place of Stress

_____

What You Were Doing

_____

Who You Were With

_____

How You Felt Physically During Your Stressful Moment

_____

_____

How You Felt Emotionally During Your Stressful Moment

_____

_____

Were You Able to Cope? Yes or No/ How Did You Cope?

_____

_____

_____

Date: _____

Stress Level Monitor During Your Day/Night

Stress Level: Calm/Medium/On the Verge/High

Time of Stress

_____

Place of Stress

_____

What You Were Doing

_____

Who You Were With

_____

How You Felt Physically During Your Stressful Moment

_____

_____

How You Felt Emotionally During Your Stressful Moment

_____

_____

Were You Able to Cope? Yes or No/ How Did You Cope?

_____

_____

_____

Date: _____

Stress Level Monitor During Your Day/Night

Stress Level: Calm/Medium/On the Verge/High

Time of Stress

_____

Place of Stress

_____

What You Were Doing

_____

Who You Were With

_____

How You Felt Physically During Your Stressful Moment

_____

_____

How You Felt Emotionally During Your Stressful
Moment

_____

_____

Were You Able to Cope? Yes or No/ How Did You
Cope? _____

_____

_____

Free Thought Page

Date_____

What You Face in Your Territory Today/Tonight:

What are you most stressed about at the start of your day/night?

_____

_____

_____

Work/Overtime/and/or Side Job o

_____

_____

_____

Caring for/Helping Someone o

_____

_____

_____

_____

Helping/Assisting Family o

_____

_____

_____

_____

Housework/Doing Errands o

_____

_____

_____

Other Tasks/Other Things You Did o

_____

_____

_____

Paying Bills o

_____

_____

Groups/Organizations/Committees o

_____

_____

_____

_____

Volunteering/Charity/Kind Acts o

_____

_____

_____

Something Good That Happened/Something You Want
to Vent About o

_____

_____

_____

_____

_____

_____

_____

_____

_____

_____

Personal Check-in

Daily Quote/Mantra/and/ or Bible Versus for
Motivation or Mood You Are In:

_____

_____

_____

_____

_____

_____

_____

Hours of Sleep You Had Last Night/Day:

_____

Was Physically Active o

_____

Ate Balanced Meals o

_____

_____

Took Prescribed Medication/Received Counseling o

_____

_____

Able to Put Money Toward Savings o

_____

Did Something Relaxing o

_____

Saw Something Amazing o

_____

Stress Level at the End of the Day/Night: Calm, Medium, On the Verge, High

What is Placing You at That Level:

_____

_____

_____

_____

_____

Other Thoughts of the Day/Night

_____

_____

_____

_____

_____

Date: _____

Stress Level Monitor During Your Day/Night

Stress Level: Calm/Medium/On the Verge/High

Time of Stress

_____

Place of Stress

_____

What You Were Doing

_____

Who You Were With

_____

How You Felt Physically During Your Stressful Moment

_____

_____

How You Felt Emotionally During Your Stressful
Moment

_____

_____

Were You Able to Cope? Yes or No/ How Did You
Cope?

_____

_____

_____

Date: _____

Stress Level Monitor During Your Day/Night

Stress Level: Calm/Medium/On the Verge/High

Time of Stress

_____

Place of Stress

_____

What You Were Doing

_____

Who You Were With

_____

How You Felt Physically During Your Stressful Moment

_____

_____

How You Felt Emotionally During Your Stressful Moment

_____

_____

Were You Able to Cope? Yes or No/ How Did You Cope?

_____

_____

_____

Date: _____

Stress Level Monitor During Your Day/Night

Stress Level: Calm/Medium/On the Verge/High

Time of Stress

_____

Place of Stress

_____

What You Were Doing

_____

Who You Were With

_____

How You Felt Physically During Your Stressful Moment

_____

_____

How You Felt Emotionally During Your Stressful Moment

_____

_____

Were You Able to Cope? Yes or No/ How Did You Cope?

_____

_____

_____

Date: _____

Stress Level Monitor During Your Day/Night

Stress Level: Calm/Medium/On the Verge/High

Time of Stress

_____

Place of Stress

_____

What You Were Doing

_____

Who You Were With

_____

How You Felt Physically During Your Stressful Moment

_____

_____

How You Felt Emotionally During Your Stressful
Moment

_____

_____

Were You Able to Cope? Yes or No/ How Did You
Cope? _____

_____

_____

Free Thought Page

Date_____

What You Face in Your Territory Today/Tonight:

What are you most stressed about at the start of your day/night?

_____

_____

_____

Work/Overtime/and/or Side Job o

_____

_____

_____

Caring for/Helping Someone o

_____

_____

_____

_____

Helping/Assisting Family o

_____

_____

_____

_____

Housework/Doing Errands o

_____

_____

_____

Other Tasks/Other Things You Did o

_____

_____

_____

Paying Bills o

_____

_____

Groups/Organizations/Committees o

_____

_____

_____

_____

_____

Volunteering/Charity/Kind Acts o

_____

_____

_____

Something Good That Happened/Something You Want
to Vent About o

_____

_____

_____

_____

_____

_____

_____

_____

_____

_____

Personal Check-in

Daily Quote/Mantra/and/ or Bible Versus for
Motivation or Mood You Are In:

_____
_____
_____
_____
_____
_____
_____
_____

Hours of Sleep You Had Last Night/Day:

_____

Was Physically Active o

_____

Ate Balanced Meals o

_____
_____

Took Prescribed Medication/Received Counseling o

_____
_____

Able to Put Money Toward Savings o

_____

Did Something Relaxing o

_____

Saw Something Amazing o

_____

Stress Level at the End of the Day/Night: Calm, Medium, On the Verge, High

What is Placing You at That Level:

_____
_____
_____
_____
_____

Other Thoughts of the Day/Night

_____
_____

_____

_____
_____

Date: _____

Stress Level Monitor During Your Day/Night

Stress Level: Calm/Medium/On the Verge/High

Time of Stress

_____

Place of Stress

_____

What You Were Doing

_____

Who You Were With

_____

How You Felt Physically During Your Stressful Moment

_____

_____

How You Felt Emotionally During Your Stressful
Moment

_____

_____

Were You Able to Cope? Yes or No/ How Did You
Cope?

_____

_____

_____

Date: _____

Stress Level Monitor During Your Day/Night

Stress Level: Calm/Medium/On the Verge/High

Time of Stress

_____

Place of Stress

_____

What You Were Doing

_____

Who You Were With

_____

How You Felt Physically During Your Stressful Moment

_____

_____

How You Felt Emotionally During Your Stressful Moment

_____

_____

Were You Able to Cope? Yes or No/ How Did You Cope?

_____

_____

_____

Date: _____

Stress Level Monitor During Your Day/Night

Stress Level: Calm/Medium/On the Verge/High

Time of Stress

_____

Place of Stress

_____

What You Were Doing

_____

Who You Were With

_____

How You Felt Physically During Your Stressful Moment

_____

_____

How You Felt Emotionally During Your Stressful
Moment

_____

_____

Were You Able to Cope? Yes or No/ How Did You
Cope?

_____

_____

_____

Date: _____

Stress Level Monitor During Your Day/Night

Stress Level: Calm/Medium/On the Verge/High

Time of Stress

_____

Place of Stress

_____

What You Were Doing

_____

Who You Were With

_____

How You Felt Physically During Your Stressful Moment

_____

_____

How You Felt Emotionally During Your Stressful
Moment

_____

_____

Were You Able to Cope? Yes or No/ How Did You
Cope? _____

_____

_____

Free Thought Page

_____

_____

_____

_____

_____

_____

_____

_____

_____

_____

_____

_____

_____

_____

_____

_____

_____

_____

_____

_____

_____

_____

_____

_____

_____

_____

_____

Date_____

What You Face in Your Territory Today/Tonight:

What are you most stressed about at the start of your day/night?

_____

_____

_____

Work/Overtime/and/or Side Job o

_____

_____

_____

Caring for/Helping Someone o

_____

_____

_____

_____

Helping/Assisting Family o

_____

_____

_____

_____

Housework/Doing Errands o

_____

_____

_____

Other Tasks/Other Things You Did o

_____

_____

_____

Paying Bills o

_____

_____

Groups/Organizations/Committees o

_____

_____

_____

_____

Volunteering/Charity/Kind Acts o

_____

_____

_____

Something Good That Happened/Something You Want to Vent About o

_____

_____

_____

_____

_____

_____

_____

_____

_____

_____

Personal Check-in

Daily Quote/Mantra/and/ or Bible Versus for Motivation or Mood You Are In:

_____

_____

_____

_____

_____

_____

_____

_____

Hours of Sleep You Had Last Night/Day:

_____

Was Physically Active o

_____

Ate Balanced Meals o

_____

_____

Took Prescribed Medication/Received Counseling o

_____

_____

Able to Put Money Toward Savings o

_____

Did Something Relaxing o

_____

Saw Something Amazing o

Stress Level at the End of the Day/Night: Calm, Medium, On the Verge, High

What is Placing You at That Level:

_____

_____

_____

_____

_____

Other Thoughts of the Day/Night

_____

_____

_____

_____

Date: _____

Stress Level Monitor During Your Day/Night

Stress Level: Calm/Medium/On the Verge/High

Time of Stress

_____

Place of Stress

_____

What You Were Doing

_____

Who You Were With

_____

How You Felt Physically During Your Stressful Moment

_____

_____

How You Felt Emotionally During Your Stressful Moment

_____

_____

Were You Able to Cope? Yes or No/ How Did You Cope?

_____

_____

_____

Date: _____

Stress Level Monitor During Your Day/Night

Stress Level: Calm/Medium/On the Verge/High

Time of Stress

_____

Place of Stress

_____

What You Were Doing

_____

Who You Were With

_____

How You Felt Physically During Your Stressful Moment

_____

_____

How You Felt Emotionally During Your Stressful Moment

_____

_____

Were You Able to Cope? Yes or No/ How Did You Cope?

_____

_____

_____

Date: _____

Stress Level Monitor During Your Day/Night

Stress Level: Calm/Medium/On the Verge/High

Time of Stress

_____

Place of Stress

_____

What You Were Doing

_____

Who You Were With

_____

How You Felt Physically During Your Stressful Moment

_____

_____

How You Felt Emotionally During Your Stressful
Moment

_____

_____

Were You Able to Cope? Yes or No/ How Did You
Cope?

_____

_____

_____

Date: _____

Stress Level Monitor During Your Day/Night

Stress Level: Calm/Medium/On the Verge/High

Time of Stress

_____

Place of Stress

_____

What You Were Doing

_____

Who You Were With

_____

How You Felt Physically During Your Stressful Moment

_____

_____

How You Felt Emotionally During Your Stressful
Moment

_____

_____

Were You Able to Cope? Yes or No/ How Did You
Cope? _____

_____

_____

Free Thought Page

_____

_____

_____

_____

_____

_____

_____

_____

_____

_____

_____

_____

_____

_____

_____

_____

_____

_____

_____

_____

_____

_____

_____

_____

_____

_____

_____

_____

_____

_____

_____

Date_____

What You Face in Your Territory Today/Tonight:

What are you most stressed about at the start of your day/night?

_____

_____

_____

Work/Overtime/and/or Side Job o

_____

_____

_____

Caring for/Helping Someone o

_____

_____

_____

_____

Helping/Assisting Family o

_____

_____

_____

_____

Housework/Doing Errands o

_____

_____

_____

Other Tasks/Other Things You Did o

_____

_____

_____

Paying Bills o

_____

_____

Groups/Organizations/Committees o

_____

_____

_____

_____

_____

Volunteering/Charity/Kind Acts o

_____

_____

_____

Something Good That Happened/Something You Want to Vent About o

_____

_____

_____

_____

_____

_____

_____

_____

_____

_____

Personal Check-in

Daily Quote/Mantra/and/ or Bible Versus for
Motivation or Mood You Are In:

_____

_____

_____

_____

_____

_____

_____

_____

Hours of Sleep You Had Last Night/Day:

_____

Was Physically Active o

_____

Ate Balanced Meals o

_____

_____

Took Prescribed Medication/Received Counseling o

_____

_____

Able to Put Money Toward Savings o

_____

Did Something Relaxing o

_____

Saw Something Amazing o

Stress Level at the End of the Day/Night: Calm, Medium, On the Verge, High

What is Placing You at That Level:

_____

_____

_____

_____

_____

Other Thoughts of the Day/Night

_____

_____

_____

_____

Date: _____

Stress Level Monitor During Your Day/Night

Stress Level: Calm/Medium/On the Verge/High

Time of Stress

_____

Place of Stress

_____

What You Were Doing

_____

Who You Were With

_____

How You Felt Physically During Your Stressful Moment

_____

_____

How You Felt Emotionally During Your Stressful Moment

_____

_____

Were You Able to Cope? Yes or No/ How Did You Cope?

_____

_____

_____

Date: _____

Stress Level Monitor During Your Day/Night

Stress Level: Calm/Medium/On the Verge/High

Time of Stress

_____

Place of Stress

_____

What You Were Doing

_____

Who You Were With

_____

How You Felt Physically During Your Stressful Moment

_____

_____

How You Felt Emotionally During Your Stressful Moment

_____

_____

Were You Able to Cope? Yes or No/ How Did You Cope?

_____

_____

_____

Date: _____

Stress Level Monitor During Your Day/Night

Stress Level: Calm/Medium/On the Verge/High

Time of Stress

_____

Place of Stress

_____

What You Were Doing

_____

Who You Were With

_____

How You Felt Physically During Your Stressful Moment

_____

_____

How You Felt Emotionally During Your Stressful Moment

_____

_____

Were You Able to Cope? Yes or No/ How Did You Cope?

_____

_____

_____

Date: _____

Stress Level Monitor During Your Day/Night

Stress Level: Calm/Medium/On the Verge/High

Time of Stress

_____

Place of Stress

_____

What You Were Doing

_____

Who You Were With

_____

How You Felt Physically During Your Stressful Moment

_____

_____

How You Felt Emotionally During Your Stressful
Moment

_____

_____

Were You Able to Cope? Yes or No/ How Did You
Cope? _____

_____

_____

Free Thought Page

_____
_____
_____
_____
_____
_____
_____
_____
_____
_____
_____
_____
_____
_____
_____
_____
_____
_____
_____
_____
_____
_____
_____
_____
_____
_____

Date_____

What You Face in Your Territory Today/Tonight:

What are you most stressed about at the start of your day/night?

_____

_____

_____

Work/Overtime/and/or Side Job o

_____

_____

_____

Caring for/Helping Someone o

_____

_____

_____

_____

Helping/Assisting Family o

_____

_____

_____

_____

Housework/Doing Errands o

_____

_____

_____

Other Tasks/Other Things You Did o

_____

_____

_____

Paying Bills o

_____

_____

Groups/Organizations/Committees o

_____

_____

_____

_____

Volunteering/Charity/Kind Acts o

_____

_____

_____

Something Good That Happened/Something You Want
to Vent About o

_____

_____

_____

_____

_____

_____

_____

_____

_____

_____

Personal Check-in

Daily Quote/Mantra/and/ or Bible Versus for Motivation or Mood You Are In:

_____

_____

_____

_____

_____

_____

_____

Hours of Sleep You Had Last Night/Day:

_____

Was Physically Active o

_____

Ate Balanced Meals o

_____

_____

Took Prescribed Medication/Received Counseling o

_____

_____

Able to Put Money Toward Savings o

_____

Did Something Relaxing o

_____

Saw Something Amazing o

_____

Stress Level at the End of the Day/Night: Calm, Medium, On the Verge, High

What is Placing You at That Level:

_____

_____

_____

_____

_____

Other Thoughts of the Day/Night

_____

_____

_____

_____

_____

Date: _____

Stress Level Monitor During Your Day/Night

Stress Level: Calm/Medium/On the Verge/High

Time of Stress

_____

Place of Stress

_____

What You Were Doing

_____

Who You Were With

_____

How You Felt Physically During Your Stressful Moment

_____

_____

How You Felt Emotionally During Your Stressful
Moment

_____

_____

Were You Able to Cope? Yes or No/ How Did You
Cope?

_____

_____

_____

Date: _____

Stress Level Monitor During Your Day/Night

Stress Level: Calm/Medium/On the Verge/High

Time of Stress

_____

Place of Stress

_____

What You Were Doing

_____

Who You Were With

_____

How You Felt Physically During Your Stressful Moment

_____

_____

How You Felt Emotionally During Your Stressful
Moment

_____

_____

Were You Able to Cope? Yes or No/ How Did You
Cope?

_____

_____

_____

Date: _____

Stress Level Monitor During Your Day/Night

Stress Level: Calm/Medium/On the Verge/High

Time of Stress

_____

Place of Stress

_____

What You Were Doing

_____

Who You Were With

_____

How You Felt Physically During Your Stressful Moment

_____

_____

How You Felt Emotionally During Your Stressful Moment

_____

_____

Were You Able to Cope? Yes or No/ How Did You Cope?

_____

_____

_____

Date: _____

Stress Level Monitor During Your Day/Night

Stress Level: Calm/Medium/On the Verge/High

Time of Stress

_____

Place of Stress

_____

What You Were Doing

_____

Who You Were With

_____

How You Felt Physically During Your Stressful Moment

_____

_____

How You Felt Emotionally During Your Stressful
Moment

_____

_____

Were You Able to Cope? Yes or No/ How Did You
Cope? _____

_____

_____

Free Thought Page

_____
_____
_____
_____
_____
_____
_____
_____
_____
_____
_____
_____
_____
_____
_____
_____
_____
_____
_____
_____
_____
_____
_____
_____
_____
_____
_____
_____
_____

Tips

*Physical Activity can combat against the increase of stress hormones and help towards issues with sleeping and aggression.

*Finding relaxation techniques is important with stress, anxiety, and anger. Meditation, breathing control (deep, slow inhale through your nose, with you imaging your spine stretching taller. Exhale slowly through your mouth), self- hypnosis (focusing on positive thoughts during a problematic issue), soothing

sounds or music, touch (like squeezing a stress ball), smell(like a soothing candle), taste (like herbal tea), and daily mantras and affirmations are a few you can try.

*Caffeine and nicotine are stimulants. Try your best to avoid them.

*If after a good night rest, you still feel fatigued or tired, drink more water.

Resources

*Mental Healthline: 1 855 552 5948

*National Domestic Violence Hotline: 1 800 799-7233

*National Suicide Prevention Lifeline/Vet Crisis Line: 1 800 273 TALK (8255),   Spanish line: 1-888-628-9454, TTY line:1 800 799 4889

*The Trevor Project-Crisis & Suicide Prevention Lifeline for LGBTQ Youth: 1 866   488 7386

*National Hopeline Network: 1 800 SUICIDE (784-2433)

*VictimConnect the National Hotline for Crime Victims: 1 855-4-Victim (1-855-484-2846)

*National Coalition of Anti-Violence Programs, National Advocacy for Local LGBT Communities:

1-212-714-1141

*National Sexual Assault Hotline: 1-800-656-4673

*Unaccompanied Alien Children (UAC) Sexual Abuse Hotline: 855 232 5393

*National Center of Elder Abuse: 1 855 500 3537

*National Council on Alcoholism and Drug Dependence, Inc.: 1 800 622 2255

*Well Spouse Association: 1 800 838 0879

*National Parent Helpline: 855 427 2736

Special thanks to my wife Michelle for your continued encouragement and love. You have made me better a person over the years. Also special thanks to my son for your motivation and your continuous growth, learning, and development, my parents for your unwavering love, support, example, and help, my parents through marriage, for your acceptance and love of me from day one, my sister and brother- in-law for your help and prayers through my life's hurtles, my aunts, uncles, and cousins for your prayers, love, support, it has been meant a lot, my sisters through marriage, thank you for all your help through the years, my other brother-in-law, thanks for checking in on me, my almost brother-in-law, thanks for everything over the years, family friends for being there during the tough times, and my God daughter and nephews for allowing me to see your growth, laughter, and wonder has been therapeutic and a joy in my life.

Thank you

Connect with me on:

Twitter- @2publications

Instagram-258mediaandpublications

Facebook-25/8 Media and Publications

Pinterest- 25/8mediaandpublications

Linkedin-d-smart-b2728b196

YOUTUBE-25 8 Media and Publications Smart

Made in the USA
Columbia, SC
17 December 2020